the flap pamphlet series

# *Paper Doll*

*open, read, turn*

# Paper Doll

the flap pamphlet series (No. 21)
Conceived in the UK, printed internationally

Published by the flap series, 2020
the pamphlet series of flipped eye publishing
All Rights Reserved

Cover Design by Petraski
Series Design © flipped eye publishing, 2010

Author Photo by Henrietta Garden
First Edition
Copyright © Katherine Lockton 2020

ISBN-13: 978-1-905233-60-1

The cover of this book features an augmented reality interpretation of the poem *On Loss* read by Katherine Lockton with augmented reality (**AR**) created by artists Scarlett Raven and Marc Marot.

> Download the free <u>Artivive</u> app from any app store and point it at the cover to unlock the **AR** beneath.

Supported using public funding by
**ARTS COUNCIL ENGLAND**
LOTTERY FUNDED

# Paper Doll

Katherine Lockton

For Nathalie and Patrick, who made me who I am

# Contents | *Paper Doll*

# On Loss

The man in the painting is not you.
The face is blurred, could belong to any
man. Probably the artist didn't know
who he painted. This doesn't stop me thinking

you have sent me flowers
I lunge into the block's industrial bin
and dig my body into waste
just to touch

flowers that you might've...
could've sent.
But you have not
sent me flowers.

Instead you sit at home,
cupped
in your wife's body. This is what it is
to lose it all. To think one thing –

to think it so real that it becomes real
just for one moment – then to see yourself
as neighbours do;
as a woman plunging into a bin.

# If We Ever Meet Again

I will wear your tweed jacket. It will rain
the way it always does when the sun is out
in Edinburgh. When the rain is done for the day

you will tell me again how amazing it is
that it rains twice; once for real and a second time
when the water caught in the trees drips

and we will laugh, and everything will be
as it should be, not a leaf out of place.
I am there now, waiting for you.

We will meet in Princes Street Gardens
and we will forgive each other: the past
and what was said no longer true.

# After Rubix

*RED*

'*Look how he steps on birds' wings,*' they say,
'*how he grabs at their feathers and makes them*
*his. If he falls it will be onto their backs*'.

'*We don't know our own bodies. I feel for my*
*thigh and find your calf, then her hip and his nose.*
*My thigh is lost somewhere between our bodies.*'

They put him in a house too small for him.
Its walls push against his ears. This is
what they had said would happen if he lied.

## What Red Does

Our aunt sits us on giant chairs and tells us to stay.
We mustn't, we shouldn't, we can't and if we do...
The tomatoes sit on their shelf untouched but bruised.

We push him in a pram too big for us to hold,
our arms grabbing only the wheels. This is what
it is to love my mother tells us; to push and push.

He doesn't know why he leans on this gate so much.
He only knows he fed the chickens here once,
feet thick with mud. Sandra, his wife, calling calling.

### What Our Parents Don't Say About Red

They painted bits of themselves red just to feel
the paint against them. It peeled off that very night
but they had felt what it was to be free.

When they no longer had a use for Miss X, they
turned her into a bike; her rear became a seat;
her neck, handles; fitted wheels on her calves.

They planted us head down, stuck us as deep
as their hands could carve into mud and rock.
They didn't know we were weeds.


### YELLOW

We bloomed in that nightly silence, danced
in its darkness. When they lit that match,
we had no use for its yellow beam.

The redness of their dance was all
we felt. Their blurred bodies moving
and moving until all we felt was them.

She threaded stones into her corset
till she could no longer move – and waited.
The potatoes turned green on their shelves.


### What Yellow Does

It lay on its belly, broken. The world
seemed bathed in white light. The only one
of its kind made like this; made to break.

The day they wed, her mum threw birdseed
at their heads for luck. When the seed fell
nearby pigeons came; eyes wide with hunger.

They hung the foal's mother, her head bowed;
as if she somehow knew to stay silent.
The men stood around in batches pointing.

## What Our Parents Don't Say About Yellow

The newborn bairns are in cots lined up
against blue walls, Hello Kittys painted
onto their feet. Outside it is raining still.

They are wearing huge glittery condoms
on their skulls and walking across Fifth Avenue
like that. They are praying, they say.

She blows bubbles as big as wild bears,
dancing to music only she hears. This time, this time,
they will take her away, her neighbours say.

## BLUE

We cover our breasts in bees. The yellow of them
comforts us. They sting as they try to suckle
this milk that was never meant for them.

With blunt scissors she chops away at the part of her
that loves him still. Her hair gone,
she contemplates cutting away at the rest.

While waiting for him to come home, she lays
herself out the way others lay out linen:
her arms, legs, chest all neatly folded.


### What Blue Does

When I find that one of me is not enough
I print eleven other versions just to see
if any number of me will ever be.

Our mother won't let us play with the neighbourhood
squirrels. Their fur is too thick, their legs
too thin. So she sends us to the sea.

The pigeons steal the newly-wed couple
in their sleep, take them above clouds
never meant for the young and drop them.


### What Our Parents Don't Say About Blue

To cigarette in the city is to laugh, mouth wide
with candy: to stare into your loved one's eyes
as they smooth you down.

Her shadow still shows the missing bits of her.
The ones she put in the washing machine
just to be rid of the smell of herself.

He puts himself into a bottle for her. At six-foot
-two his feet stick out. The way they always did
in bed. She uses his shoes to push him down.

GREEN

We lie in bed as close as dominoes,
ball bearings digging into our hips. This is what it's like
to lose you over and over again.

You have taken my bed and spread your golden locks
across my pillow. The porridge I make for you
is too hot, too cold and never just right.

I dreamt you were amongst the stars,
your reflection falling into waves. My body pressed
against your light, as I fumbled the water's darkness.

## What Green Does

The shed you build in your garden
is wonky, the door skewing to one side.
All I want to do is to live inside its walls.

You turn me over like an avocado past its best.
I am the bride who became frightened of life opened
before her eyes. My flesh no longer mine.

You carve yourself into my body. I watch from the ceiling.
I watch myself watching myself looking at us,
the two mes: the one before you and the one after.

## What Our Parents Don't Say About Green

I am drawing a line between us in bed.
The marker fades as I press down into the sheets.
You tell me that there never will be another pen,

that this too is the last of the ink, and that I must make do,
before turning my hand away, and scrunching it into a fist.
When I can't sleep I give Selima's men breasts.

I dress them in my old leotard. They arch their backs,
but do not fall into her water. Instead
they bend themselves back onto spikes and laugh.


ORANGE

You make prints of my breasts, hand them
out to your friends. This is only to be expected,
your wife says, slamming your door on me.

I give you a box you can't refuse, but the paper is too tight.
Your nails break against its wrapping paper.
Your wife tends the wounds you tell her nettles have caused.

Yet again my wet nurse wakes me from dreams of you.
Her fist clangs my door. Virginia died this way.
The weight of the stones carried her to her wet nurse.


## What Orange Does

I have become obsessed with drawing houses for us
to live in. With each house I draw, the hunger
for our happily ever after grows until it is a shadow of my bed.

Your face blurs at times under the darkness but I know
it is still you whose arms I want to die in.
When I hear of your demise I watch from the back of the church,

dressed in blue. It would have been easier for us
if we had been made from the same dirt.
We are both hungry for what the other has.


## What Our Parents Don't Say About Orange

The tunnel was dim. And I grew afraid
of the dark. You held my head to your chest,
the beat of your heart comforting me.

You are not Frida. Who said you were?
You are anything but her for she is me and I am her.
Marry yourself then. You have married everyone else.

To clean yourself for her you have strung me up
like a scarecrow. Her curls are still intact.
The ribs of my corset show hips that will never bear young.


## WHITE

She tied a noose to hang me by, then made me hang myself.
The rope was too loose to choke me, too tight to let me go.
I hung there like a warning to others that would come after me.

I traumatised a generation of Bolivian women,
so they never had daughters and never opened windows.
It was my fault watermelons never ripened in their hips.

My trip to the Americas is married with hate.
The image of you burns into my womb.
All I can do is watch.

## What White Does

I am growing old in your sweat.
The skin beneath my breasts creasing from your years
with her. I shall forget what it is to want.

The water is unforgiving, it drags you under.
It will not let you play with it, the way a baby plays
in its tiny bath those first months.

With you I want to be brave enough to give up,
to be like a duckling swimming
in its first rain, just letting go.


## What Our Parents Don't Say About White

Britain is my home, it built me the way Geppetto
built Pinocchio, limb by limb with pure love.
You took it all then left without looking back.

It's the not knowing which makes me wake again
to love you. Let a corset of my bones wrap
round her like a fist. Then let her sing of love.

I am sorry. Sorry for the blankness.
Sometimes you have to turn all that love
to hate, just to survive.

# Mi Lengua

Mientras comia mi cereal esta manana
While eating my cereal this morning
se cayo mi lengua en mi plato. Se quedo ahí
my tongue fell off into my plate. It stayed there
nadando en la leche mientras mi mama me hablaba.
swimming in milk while my mum spoke.
No he podido decirle que no puedo hablar.
I couldn't tell her that I could no longer speak.
En ese momento lluegue a entender que la vida
In that moment I understood that life
pasa mientras que nosotras las mujeres planchamos
passes us by while us women iron
the shirts of our men.
las camisas de nuestros hombres.

# Platanos Partidos

Al caerse, On falling, la nina se despierta en un mundo hecho de caras que rien. the girl wakes to a world made of faces that laugh. Sus bocas abiertas, como platanos partidos; Their mouths open, like split bananas; clowns of the night, payasos de la noche. Here where no one talks like her, Aqui donde nadie habla como ella, the people sleep during the day, and happiness is bought with a bag of sweets. la gente duerme durante el dia y la felicidad se compra con una bolsa de dulces. Her life; a soap opera that never ends, with episodes, one after another, that fall away like dominoes. Su vida; una novella interminable, con episodios, uno tras otro, que caen como dominos. "¿Es 'Is esta, this life?' la vida?" "Reirse 'To laugh mientras while el mundo se revuelve como un loco encarselado en una caja golpeando las paredes?" the world turns itself around like a madman locked up in a box bashing the walls?' the woman made from the little girl that fell, pregunta asks la mujer fue echa de la nina que cayo, asks the woman made from the little girl that fell.

# Dreams of Falling

My mami wraps me in an aguayo,
packs me into its colours as tightly
as meat tucked into an empanada.
She pulls up her pollera, then throws
me from my aunt's seventh floor window.
She does this because I'll fall anyway.

I fall towards my brother in London.
I fall for the sweet seller's baby.
I follow her down the street as I fall.
I am as small as my mother's only doll
whose head broke off and never got fixed.

# Reading My Skin

On my left thigh you touch *sad*,
on my right *lonely*:
your finger presses down
as if to double-check.

Stroking the inside of my legs,
you find *broken*, then travel to my belly,
pausing at *Bolivian* and *English* – confused.
It's not till you touch *perdida*
that you begin to understand my unease.

On my soles you tickle *fall, Tarija*
near the number *four*.

At the bend of my knees *Huntsville,*
*Texas* where you stop for five seconds,
tapping on *strangers*, *religion* and *home*
where I try to nudge your fingers away.

But you linger longer, almost a minute
at my hip bone, on *New York, Joe, John*
and a word even you won't say aloud.

You begin to realise why
I was reluctant to be read.

On the rise of my left breast – at *Edinburgh*
and *tha gaol agam ort* – you stop:
not wanting or needing
to feel anymore.

# The Angle

From this angle you can only see what she sees,
the button on his trousers as he undresses to pee.
The metallic tuppence-like shine and the words Levi's.
There is no mistaking the scene. She is scrunched
into a three-and-a-half-year old ball; kneeling down,
looking up, waiting for her turn to pee. Then he turns,
faces her and tries to enter her as if she were a tunnel
and him a car. She stares at the smooth white door.
Then, as if God somehow knew to call *cut,* there is
banging and shouting. The director walks away
hands buried deep inside his pockets.

## Being Alice

I wanted to be smaller
so I cut my paper dolls
~~and me~~
but still they came

those girls who called me

names
and kicked

I wanted to be bigger
to kick back so I had seconds
and ate bread

but then the men came

so I started to shrink again,

but the men
they came back
hungrier

then I realised
I just had to
become who
I already was

# Playing with Dolls

When they hand me my doll, I hide
the way toddlers seek refuge
behind the veils of their mothers' skirts.

It has wiry pubic hair. I tell them I do not recall ever seeing his.
That I froze as he released himself between my thighs.
This is what happens when you talk

to or look at married men. I show them
how his eyes closed as he came.

And how I begged then froze.

I hate my doll-body, so I pile on layers
to hide what was already hidden.
I take soap to her dirty skin.

Wash after wash I feel her unease grow.
I will never be able to rid her of your grip,
your lips against her nipples.

It is not her fault she is pretty
that your hands trap her hips
as she begs you to stop.

She tells you, you are betraying your wife
that what you take now is not yours.
When you are done she cries.

So many nights I will spend crying, at the sight of you,
and at my failure to stop you.
She tells myself that she crossed that river
so that I would not. That when she folded
herself into him she was unfurling me
from men like that.

I hate looking at my reflection; I only see
his fingers suspended in glass –
there, but somehow not there.

# The Rape Scene

**1**

How do you say to someone that they have been living
in the wrong house. That a home is not somewhere
you are scared to be and that not all men lie, use
and abuse you. One day you will learn that
how you grew up was not like everyone else,
there was never anything you could do
to stop what happened. You will learn
there is no background music to a rape scene.

**2**

There is no special lighting when he grabs at you
yanking your jeans and underwear down.
The director hasn't spent hours fiddling
with undertones, props and fixtures.
Neither has the rapist. He is just here.
There is just a car with car seats
or the National Theatre with the river
in the background. The same place
you used to want to be married in,
the place where your sister wanted to be
married – the place he has made a rape scene.

**3**

He tries to hold your hand in the café
you say *no* firmly, say that you are leaving
but he says sorry, he won't do it again.

**4**

He whispers in your ear while you dance
at his sister's wedding. Later your mother,
the woman who brought you into this world,
heard your first scream and your heart first
beat against hers, the woman you love,
will refer to that night as the night
you got off with the bride's brother.

**5**

Your cousin.
Your ex's friend.

**6**

Music is playing in his car. He is drunk and driving
you home. He pulls in
and you panic.

**7**

You ripped your dress so you wouldn't have to
go to the wedding. You sensed the danger
coming. Your angry mother in the bathroom
with your sister. You bang on the door
when he first gives you that look, the I want to
fuck you look. So you tear your dress.
Your mother, annoyed, hands you another.

**8**

He pulls his car in and you can already see
what is happening as it happens because it does
happen.

**9**

There is no music playing in the background
of the rape scene; even though there is
you can't hear it. You are somewhere else.

**10**

You ask yourself what is a rape anyway?
A finger? A mouth? A .....................

**11**

Afterwards you say to yourself it must be your fault.
That it can't have happened. Not twice.
Not to you.

**12**

How can it be his fault? He/they has/have a mother. A wife.
A daughter and son.

**13**

Your mother says it isn't rape
because he is younger than you.
Did you rape him?

**14**

Why did you protect him? When people looked
why did you cover your eyes so they couldn't see
the pain? Why did you kiss his forehead,
the rapist's forehead, the next morning
as his mother looked on smiling as he slept

on your bed, still apparently drunk,
you suddenly sober from the truth?

**15**

Why did you kiss his forehead as he slept?

**16**

You shout and scream at him at the foot of the stairs.
He wants to hug you. You don't let him.
Instead you walk away. Get the bus home
and don't tell anyone. How can you?

**17**

You imagine your ex talking to him. Then
you realise you can never tell anyone.

**18**

And why did you – six months later – accuse
your father instead, then hide in a mental hospital;
the only place you felt safe, the only place
you feel safe even now?

**19**

You see someone slit their neck with plastic.
But still this is better. To be safe. Here.

**20**

Why do you continue to protect him/them?

**21**

Because you don't want to create a scene.

A rape scene. With a white-chalk outline
of your body. Now someone else's body.

Even though you said no or couldn't say no.

Even though you said no more times that night
than you have ever said yes in your life.

# In Praise of the Washing Machine

Then one day they came out in the laundry.
All those colours I tried so hard to hide.

# Incommunicado, Tate Modern

I find the tiny steel structure after the third miscarriage,
tucked in a corner. It calls out to me.
Heavily lit and engulfed by white space,
it lies remote and confused,
craving something it doesn't understand.

David says *it's meant to symbolize some sort of prison.*
I whisper to the sculpture *what do you want?*
The sculpture is shiny, hollow and sharp.
I run my fingers across its mesh.
*I would put my baby in you.*

# Blue Grapes

*after Henri Cole*

You are sorry you cannot say you love me
when I say *I love you*.
My words are fat grapes you love to eat,
fingers still sticky with honey
and white from cheese.

I lie on my back, humming blue
as you apply red to your lips.
Our marriage is a continuous performance.

In Moscow you are everything a lover should be.
*I was being selfish* is your answer to all my questions
and pleas for you to love me back;
as if you could ever love me,
as if anyone could ever love me.

The lipstick smudges when we kiss.
Time's sharp pointed legs
dig into my thighs.

The man who tries to slide his fingers
inside me when I fall asleep on a bus
stops me telling you how I hate for my stomach
to be rubbed, that I prefer you to kiss me
as if you were kissing a prostitute and that sometimes
I just want to sleep.

# Questions

What will the butcher's wife say of me
after tomorrow morning, when she takes over the shop floor
from her husband, baby in her arms, her man shuffling upstairs to rest?
Will she say: *that woman; the one who comes here for chicken
thighs. Why does she not come?* How will they know of you?
How will anyone know that the reason I leave it all
is you?

# The Wishbone

He presents her/ with my carcass/ stuffed/
with fruit-chestnut /on their first dinner date;/

whispering, *'what is mine /is yours'* into her ear.
The chef has shaved/ my limbs into bite-sized

diamonds for her petite mouth./ I bleed cranberry./
A crack vibrates through the room/ as they make a wish

together./ *'What is mine is yours,'*/ he whispers into her ear,/
dabbing the corners of her mouth/ for her with my skin.

# Sweat

I roll to an empty side
to find nothing but the smell of crotch
still with me in the morning

The sheets are stiff as the starched
shirts of new police recruits.

I move my hand between my legs
feel the dampness of another wet dream;
mating with Gods:
Zeus, Apollo and Dionysus.

Or I am Penelope testing suitors,
ten men suckling my breasts
one nibbling at my ear.

Some mornings I am Athena
with Odysseus, I am Penelope
with Agamemnon, but never Penelope
with Odysseus.

# The Plastic Princess

*Me as Your Blow Up Doll*

As you inflate my ribs,
lips tucked
into my x
your hands wander
up to my waist. I am
to be your fantasy

and you will
bend me, like the ballerina
I once was. You tell me I am
the thing that makes you
most alive. You blow,

watch as my back unfurls,
firm with life: a loud PFFT
followed by a squeak
as you seal me shut

the only way you can.


*Me as Your Vinyl Doll*

You dress us in outfits that clash
with one another to make a point.

Placing us on stools, you position plastic
cups filled with make-believe tea
beside the shiny cookies before us

though we can't move to drink. I study
my plastic belly, then your wife's sparkly
dress, chequered tights and red coat covering
stretch marks you have given her.

*Me as Your Doll of Wires*

You gather hay, wire and clay, opting
to start by sculpting my feet from wire mesh.
The wire dyes pink creases into your pale skin.

Folding hay into its corners and dipping me in clay
ensures my body will last you five years.
Your hands mould my hips, breasts and tongue.

You work slowly, smoothing me down; once
I am finished you know you can live without me.
You are happy with your wife: always

dieting but never losing weight. She makes you feel
enough, your flesh is firm against her loose skin.
Plus, you say, *there are 364 others*

*like me willing to line up outside* your shed.
They are younger, stretchier, dumber – and happier
to play at being your shadow: hiding, then seeking you out.

## Me as Your Wardrobe Doll

My make-believe, shoulda,
coulda had three children swing
in my wardrobe, next to *that* red dress.
They are lined up with my shoulda,
coulda, husband Adam.
They sit next to a burning fire.
Eve, the youngest, plays
piano keys that cackle
like bones breaking
as I sew their school uniforms.

# The Fire Alarm

I decide to pull the alarm
before the fire has started
before it is too late for us all.
Now my body is full with the fumes
that could have been. And I am
lost in white fog.

# Paper Dolls

You keep me folded in the inside pocket
of your coat like a dirty secret glanced at
only when your wife is too busy.

I am going yellow at the edges.
The last time you checked on me
there was a slight tear by my right thigh.

I hold hands with another girl
whose body is bent against mine.
She is just one in a long queue.

Pressed up against me, the dolls
feel the rip in me. The fright
of it makes them tear themselves

like women who have given birth.

# The Snow Globe

I find myself looking through your emails,
farming the history of us for love
something that was never there to grow.
I shovel the messages into the dirt

hoping something other than sadness will grow
from remnants mixed with ash.
I remember the wind blew, the dog howled
I recall the heat. Oh! and those trees!

The whisper of their leaves mixed
with sweet nothings. Do you remember
the heat as I lay on you?
The whole world closing around us.

# The Paper Doll Chain

I am cutting her and her sisters from paper
that my sister has given me. The scissors score
across her pencil outline. One day I will become
this paper doll. I will have her skirt, thighs
and breasts that I will always think are too big.
I will try and cut her again and keep her safe
by making her smaller, and I will want to keep her
in a box. But she will defy me; time after time
teaching me how to live when she does.

# What Love Really Is

Here I am by the ledge.

The crowd beneath not formed.
I have a fever and lie in bed dreaming.

The swan that will fly beneath me
to break my fall is opening his wings.

He tries to curl his tongue around the words *nina, caer*
to call out. But all the passersby hear is his chafing voice.

Our front door slams. Startled I call *mamita,* and lean out.
I wake to find my whole world changed:

my floor, the walls, even my sheets, the mute colour
of earth. My swan curls his neck, head pressed to my left foot.

When I am older I will forget this shade of brown
forget that the colour of pain is the colour of life.

When I am older I will forget this shade of brown
forget that the colour of life is the colour of pain

my floor, the walls, even my sheets are the mute colour
of earth. My swan curls his neck, head pressed to my right foot.

Our front door slams. Startled I call *mamita,* and lean out.
I wake to find my whole world changed.

45

He tries to uncurl his tongue around the words *hidden, secret*
to call out. But all the passersby hear is his chafing voice.

The swan that will refuse to fly beneath me
to break my fall is opening his wings.

The crowd beneath has not formed.
I have a fever and lie in bed dreaming.

Here I am by the ledge.

# Paper Doll Sisters

My sisters and I are connected like paper dolls.
No one can see where the paper folds

between our bodies, though they feel
the weight of the others when they tug at one of us.

They say we are strong Latin women
who hold themselves like men.

They don't know it is the other women that hold us
in place the whole time we refuse to move.

it is because the other women refuse to budge.